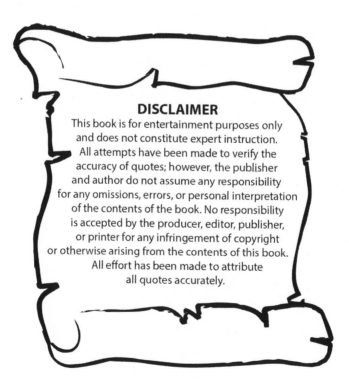

***Motivated Teen:***
***300 Unique Quotes For Living A Confident Life***
is a beautiful collection of inspirational words from
famous and everyday people.

**Life's a gift. Live it wisely. Live it best.**
**Pixinspired.com**

Try to be like

the **TURTLE**

at ease
in your own shell.

Bill Copeland

Each day provides its own GIFTS.

Marcus Aurelius

shoot for the **moon** and if you miss you will still be among the stars.

**Les Brown**

No act of **Kindness,**

no matter how small,

is ever wasted.

Aesop

The power of
imagination
makes us infinite.

John Muir

We can't HELP
everyone,
but everyone can help
someone.

Ronald Reagan

Out of difficulties grow
*miracles.*

Jean de la Bruyere

What we **think**, we become.

Buddha

There is

a **PLAN** and a **PURPOSE**,
a value to every life,
no matter what its location,
AGE,
GENDER
or DISABILITY.

**Sharron Angle**

**Life** is
what happens
while you are busy
making other
plans.

John Lennon

# BE

# Grateful♡

## FOR ALL YOU HAVE
even when it seems like nothing.

Adaeze A.E

Always desire to *Learn* something useful.

Sophocles

attribute my success
to this – I never gave or
took any excuse.

Florence Nightingale

The **key** is to keep company only with people who uplift you, whose presence calls forth your best.

Epictetus

Look up at the **STARS**
and not down at your feet.
Try to make sense of
what you see,
and wonder about
what makes
the universe exist.

Be Curious.

Stephen Hawking

If you can **Dream** it,
you can do it.

**Walt Disney**

In order to succeed,
we must first

**Believe**

that we can.

**Nikos Kazantzakis**

Only I can change my life.
No one can do it for me.

Carol Burnett

I see
myself
as the best
**footballer**
in the world.
If you don't believe
you are the best,
then you will never achieve
all that you are capable of.

**Cristiano Ronaldo**

THE **SINGLE** MOST POWERFUL THING I CAN BE IS TO BE MYSELF.

Dwayne Johnson

The biggest competition
is myself.
I am not looking to follow others
or pull them down.
I'm planning to test
my own boundaries.

**Rain**

Everyone has
# highs and lows
that they have to learn from,
but every morning
I start off with a good head
on my shoulders,
saying to myself,
'It's going to be a good day!'.

Lindsay Lohan

Life is not a solo act.
It's a huge collaboration,
and we all need to assemble

around us the people
who care about us
and support us
in times of strife.

**Tim Gunn**

Step with care
and great tact,
and remember that Life's
a **GREAT** **BALANCING** Act.

**Dr. Seuss**

For every good reason there is to **Lie,** there is a better reason to tell the **Truth.**

Bo Bennett

To be trusted is a greater compliment than being Loved.

George MacDonald

Surround yourself with
really good people.
I think that's an important thing.
**Because the people
you surround yourself
are a reflection of you.**

**Aaron Rodgers**

It's **cool** to be different and just be who you are and shock people in a **good way.**

Brendon Urie

I think;
therefore I am.

Rene Descartes

WHEN I AM
MYSELF,
I AM
HAPPY AND HAVE A
GOOD RESULT.

Jack Ma

I don't want other people to decide who I am.

I want to decide that for myself.

Emma Watson

I take a lot of

# PRIDE

in being myself.
I'm comfortable
with who I am.

**James McAvoy**

IF YOU TAKE
RESPONSIBILITY FOR YOURSELF
YOU WILL DEVELOP
A HUNGER TO ACCOMPLISH
YOUR
DREAMS.

**Les Brown**

Share your **smile** with the world. It's a symbol of friendship and peace.

Christie Brinkley

Everything is a learning process: any time

you **fall** over, it's just teaching you to stand up the next time.

**Joel Edgerton**

Do not mind anything
that anyone tells you
about anyone else.
Judge
everyone and everything
for yourself.

Henry James

# POSITIVE THINKING
will let you do everything better
than negative thinking will.

**Zig Ziglar**

The mind is everything.
What you think you

BECOME.

**Buddha**

# Family

is not an important thing.

It's everything.

Michael J. Fox

To be one,
to be united is a great thing.
But to respect
the right to be different
is maybe even
GREATER.

**Bono**

Your peers will respect you for your integrity and character, not your possessions.

David Robinson

Different people
have different opinions,
and it's okay
to respect all of them.

Juan Pablo Galavis

We may be divided by history but we are united by

# humanity.

Meso E

We don't need to share
the same opinions as others,
but we need to be

# RESPECTFUL.

**Taylor Swift**

Respect your efforts,
respect yourself.
Self-respect leads

to self-discipline.
When you have both firmly
under your belt,
that's real power.

Clint Eastwood

# Treat everyone
## with respect and kindness.
## PERIOD.
## NO EXCEPTIONS.

Kiana Tom

Responsibility for learning belongs to the student, regardless of age.

Robert Martin

## Work hard, be kind,

and amazing things will happen.

Conan O'Brien

# Believe in yourself,
### and the rest
### will fall into place.

Have faith in your own abilities,
# work hard,
### and there is nothing
### you cannot accomplish.

**Brad Henry**

SELF—BELIEF & HARD WORK
WILL ALWAYS EARN YOU
SUCCESS.

**Virat Kohli**

Every day brings
# NEW CHOICES.

Martha Beck

Whenever you have
taken up work in hand,
you must see it to the finish.
That is the ultimate secret of success.

Never,
Never,
Never
Give Up!

**Dada Vaswani**

**My message is:**
You don't have to give up
being popular,
fun,
or fashionable
in order to be smart;
they can go hand and hand.
Doing math is a great way
to exercise your brain;
being smart
is going to make you
more powerful in life.

Danica McKellar

**Beauty** is about perception, not about make-up. I think the beginning of all beauty is knowing and liking oneself. You can't put on make-up, or dress yourself, or do you hair with any sort of fun or joy if you're doing it from a position of correction.

Kevyn Aucoin

Being nice is awesome.
**You have**
**more fun;**
**you meet**
**more people.**

**Charli XCX**

The important thing is to learn
a lesson every time you lose.
Life is a learning process
and you have to try to learn
what's best for you.
Let me tell you,

# life is not fun

when you're banging your head
against a brick wall all the time.

**John McEnroe**

There's no need
to dress like everyone else.

It's much more FUN
to create your
own look.

**Twiggy**

Adolescence isn't just about prom or wearing sparkly dresses.

Jena Malone

The only way
to have a **friend**
is to be one.

**Ralph Waldo Emerson**

# No one succeeds
### without effort...
### Those who succeed
### owe their success
## to perseverance.

Ramana Maharshi

**Life** is not
easy for any of us.
But what of that?
We must have perseverance
and above all confidence
in **ourselves.**
We must believe that
we are gifted for something
and that this thing must be
Attained.

Marie Curie

And so you touch this limit,
something happens
and you suddenly can go
a little bit further.
With your **mind power**,
your **determination**,
your **instinct**,
and the **experience** as well,

you can fly very

High.

Ayrton Senna

The price of success is hard work,
dedication to the job at hand,

and the Determination
that whether we win or lose,
we have applied
the best of ourselves
to the task at hand.

**Vince Lombardi**

Try to make
at least one person
happy every day.

If you cannot do a **KIND** deed,
speak a kind word.
If you cannot speak a kind word,
think a kind thought.

**Count up**, if you can,
the treasure of happiness that
you would dispense in a week,
in a year, in a lifetime!

Lawrence G. Lovasik

Mistakes are always
forgivable,
if one has the courage
to admit them.

Bruce Lee

I THINK THERE'S A TIME
IN YOUR LIFE
WHERE YOU DON'T FEEL LIKE
**YOU FIT IN.**
I THINK EVERYONE HAS THAT
WHEN YOU'RE A TEENAGER,
ESPECIALLY,
AND
ESPECIALLY IN THE SOCIETY
WE LIVE IN.

Matthew Vaughn

I love being
**TEEN**
a
because you don't have
all the responsibilities
of an adult yet.

**Elizabeth Gillies**

My teenage years
were exactly what they were
supposed to be.
Everybody has their own path.
It's laid out for you.
It's just up to you to walk it.

**Justin Timberlake**

Being a **TEEN**
can be tough.
Just try to surround yourself
with really good friends
that really have your back,
and also be a really good friend
to those who really care about you.

If you're not sure
about certain things,
talk to your friends that
you trust and your family.

Victoria Justice

# Being a teenager

is an amazing time
and a hard time.
It's when you make
your best friends - I have girls
who will never leave my heart
and I still talk to.
You get the best and the worst

## as a teen.

You have the best friendships
and the worst
heartbreaks.

Sophia Bush

Good habits
formed at youth make all the

# DIFFERENCE.

**Aristotle**

It takes courage
to grow up and become
who you
really are.

e. e. cummings

# I never cut class.

I loved getting A's,
I liked being smart.
I liked being on time.

# I thought being smart is cooler than anything in the world.

**Michelle Obama**

*Every minute of every hour*
*of every day*

you are making the world,
just as you are making yourself,
and you might as well do it with
generosity and kindness and style.

**Rebecca Solnit**

Bad things do happen in the world,

# like war,

natural disasters,

disease.

But out of those situations

always arise stories of

ordinary people doing

## extraordinary things.

**Daryn Kagan**

COUNT YOUR

BLESSINGS.

YOU ARE ONE OF A KIND.

THERE'S NO ONE IN THE WORLD

LIKE YOU.

YOU ARE AMAZING.

**Richard Simmons**

# Being Different

gives the world color.

Nelsan Ellis

If you're you, it doesn't matter if you're the most **boring person** in the world: someone will **like you.** You're not trying to be anyone else.

Lil Uzi Vert

Character is doing the right thing

when **nobody's looking.**
There are too many people
who think that the only thing
that's right is to get by,
and the only thing
that's wrong is to get caught.

J. C. Watts

**Life**

doesn't require that
we be the best,
only that we try our best.

H. Jackson Brown, Jr.

Picking
a best friend
who stands up
for what she believes in,
is true to herself and allows you
to be yourself
without judgement
of how 'cool' you are?
Well, now you're picking
a friend for life.

Renee Olstead

The best way
to cheer yourself up
is to try
to cheer
somebody
else up.

Mark Twain

I follow three rules:
*Do the right thing,
do the best you can,
and
always show people you care.*

**Lou Holtz**

When we seek to
# DISCOVER
the best in others,
we somehow bring out
the best in ourselves.

**William Arthur Ward**

I think every girl needs to **love** herself, regardless of anything. Like if you're having a bad day, if you don't like your hair, if you don't have the best **family situation,** whatever, you have to love yourself and you can't do anything until you love yourself first.

Julianne Hough

*I don't know the key to success,* BUT THE KEY TO FAILURE IS TRYING TO PLEASE EVERYBODY.

Bill Cosby

**Focused,** hard work is the real key to success. Keep your eyes on the goal, and just keep taking the next step towards completing it. If you aren't sure which way to do something, **do it both ways** and see which works better.

ABCD

It's not the situation,
but whether
we react
NEGATIVE OR RESPOND POSITIVE
to the situation
that is important.

**Zig Ziglar**

Your DESTINY is to
fulfill those things
upon which you focus most intently.
So choose to keep your focus
on that which is truly magnificent,
beautiful, uplifting and joyful.
Your life is always moving toward something.

**Ralph Marston**

In every day,
there are **1,440 minutes.**
That means
we have 1,440 daily opportunities
to make a positive impact.

**Les Brown**

Your body is
your body;
it's natural.
Learn to
love yourself for it.

Emily Ratajkowski

Your **self-esteem** won't come from body parts. You need to step away from the mirror every once in a while,

and look for **another reflection,** like the one in the eyes of the people who love you and admire you.

**Stacy London**

You've got to

**love** yourself first.
You've got to be okay on your own
before you can be okay
with somebody else.

Jennifer Lopez

You can search throughout
the entire universe for someone
who is more deserving of your love and affection
than you are yourself,
and that person is not to be found anywhere.
You yourself,
as much as anybody in the entire universe
deserve your love and affection.

Buddha

Be happy with being you.
LOVE YOUR FLAWS.
OWN YOUR QUIRKS.

And know that you are just
as perfect as anyone else,
exactly as you are.

**Ariana Grande**

One way to feel good
about yourself is to
**LOVE**
yourself...
to take care of yourself.

Goldie Hawn

Don't just be alive.

Be in life.

Zara E

# Friends can help each other.
A true friend is
someone who lets you
have total freedom
to be yourself – and especially to feel.
Or, not feel.
Whatever you happen to be feeling
at the moment is fine with them.
That's what real love
amounts to – letting a person
be what he really is.

**Jim Morrison**

**Beauty is**
when you can appreciate yourself.
When you love yourself,
that's when you're most beautiful.

Zoe Kravitz

# FRIENDS

show their love
in times of trouble,
not in happiness.

**Euripides**

I don't want to be
linked to anything negative.
I don't want
   negative energy.
I want everything

positive around me.

Kendra Wilkinson

Having a **POSITIVE** mental attitude is asking how something can be **Done** rather than saying it can't be done.

**Bo Bennett**

I HAVE LEARNED THAT

# CHAMPIONS

AREN'T JUST BORN;
CHAMPIONS CAN BE MADE
WHEN THEY EMBRACE AND COMMIT

TO LIFE—CHANGING

POSITIVE HABITS.

**Lewis Howes**

It takes but one positive thought
when given
a **chance** to
survive and thrive
to overpower an entire army of
negative thoughts.

Robert H. Schuller

Your **smile**
will give you
a positive countenance
that will make people feel
comfortable around you.

Les Brown

W<small>E</small> M<small>AKE</small>
# THE WORLD
W<small>E</small> L<small>IVE</small> I<small>N AND</small> S<small>HAPE</small>
O<small>UR</small> O<small>WN</small> E<small>NVIRONMENT.</small>

**Orison Swett Marden**

If you don't **ask,**
you don't get.

Stevie Wonder

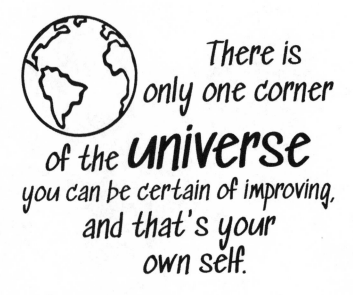

There is
only one corner
of the **universe**
you can be certain of improving,
and that's your
own self.

**Aldous Huxley**

 Be kind

whenever possible.

It is always possible.

Dalai Lama

The will to win,
the desire to succeed,
the urge to reach your full potential...

these are the keys that will unlock
the door to personal excellence.

Confucius

# I BELIEVE

THAT ANYONE CAN BE
WHAT THEY WANT TO BE;
IT JUST COMES DOWN
TO HARD WORK.

Kiesza

# I GUARANTEE

THE PEOPLE WHO STUDY ARE GOING TO BE SUCCESSFUL.

## NOTHING CAN REPLACE HARD WORK.

Freeman A. Hrabowski III

I know you've heard it
a thousand times before.
But it's true
hard work pays off.
If you want to be good,
you have to practice, practice, practice.
If you don't love something,
then don't do it.

Ray Bradbury

# EMOTIONAL SELF-CONTROL

is the result of hard work,
not an inherent skill.

Travis Bradberry

# You need three things to win:

discipline,
hard work and,
before everything maybe,
commitment.

No one will make it without those three.

## Sport teaches you that.

Haile Gebrselassie

# Plans are
only good intentions
unless they immediately
degenerate
into hard work.

Peter Drucker

That's the thing
about awards - it's for the people
who do all the hard work
behind the scenes.
An award is just
a clap at them.

Sia

You just have to find that
thing that's special about you
that **distinguishes** you
from all the others,
and through true talent,
**hard work,**
and **passion,**
anything can happen.

**Dr. Dre**

*Freedom* is nothing
but a chance
to be better.

Albert Camus

Wisdom, Compassion, and Courage

are the **3** universally recognized moral qualities of men.

Confucius

The more you like yourself,
the less you are like anyone else,
which makes you

# UNIQUE

**Walt Disney**

# Change

what you can,
and don't let
what you can't change
weigh you down

Adaeze A.E

The journey
of a thousand miles
begins with
one **step.**

Lao Tzu

It takes a
great deal of bravery
to stand up
to our **enemies,**
but just as much to stand up
to our **friends.**

J. K. Rowling

# FRIENDS...

## THEY CHERISH
## ONE ANOTHER'S HOPES.
## THEY ARE KIND
## TO ONE ANOTHER'S DREAMS.

Henry David Thoreau

You have power over
your mind - not outside
events.
Realize this,
and you will find
strength.

Marcus Aurelius

Passion is energy.
FEEL THE POWER
that comes from
focusing
on what excites you.

**Oprah Winfrey**

The past cannot be

# CHANGED.

The future is yet
in your power.

Unknown

Think of **success** as a game of chance in which you have control over the odds. As you begin to master concepts in personal achievement, you are increasing your odds of achieving success.

**Bo Bennett**

LEARNING TO **TRUST** IS ONE OF LIFE'S MOST DIFFICULT TASKS.

Isaac Watts

I learned the value
of hard work
by
**working hard.**

Margaret Mead

Know the true value of
**time;**
*snatch,*
*seize,*
and enjoy
every moment of it.
No idleness, no laziness,
no procrastination:
never put off till tomorrow
what you can do today.

Philip Stanhope, 4th Earl of Chesterfield

The future starts today, not tomorrow.

Pope John Paul II

I believe that every single one of us,
celebrity or not,
has a responsibility
to get involved in trying to make

a **difference in the world.**
Our generation faces many challenges,
some of which were passed
on to us by the past generations,
but it's up to us
to find solutions today
so that we don't keep passing
our problems on.

Shakira

The future belongs to those who prepare for it
today.

Malcolm X

Don't ever doubt yourselves or waste a second of your life. It's too short, and you're too special.

Ariana Grande

I feel that the *simplicity* of life is just being yourself.

Bobby Brown

Too often we underestimate
the power of
a touch,
a smile,
a kind word,
a listening ear,
an honest compliment,
or the smallest act of caring,
all of which have the potential
to turn a life around.

**Leo Buscaglia**

The purpose
of human life is to serve,
and to show compassion
and the will to
help others.

**Albert Schweitzer**

Stay true to yourself,
yet always be open to learn.
**Work hard,**
and never give up on your dreams,
even when nobody else believes
they can come true but you.

These are not cliches
but real tools you need no matter
what you do in life
to stay focused on your path.

**Phillip Sweet**

Find something
that you're really interested in
doing in your life.
**PURSUE IT,**
**SET GOALS,**
**AND**
**COMMIT YOURSELF**
to excellence.
Do the best you can.

**Chris Evert**

I believe that in life,
you have to give things
your best shot,
do your best.
You have to focus on
what needs to be done,
do the right thing,
not the popular thing.

**David Cameron**

I genuinely
want to do my best
**every day,**
and I genuinely want to enjoy life
**every day.**

**Landon Donovan**

# The best way

to survive life is - never fret over

what you don't get.

There's a

bigger

plan for you.

**Shilpa Shetty**

Being the best
at whatever talent you have,
that's what stimulates

life

Tom Landry

I would like to be

# remembered

as someone

who did the best

she could with

the talent she had.

J. K. Rowling

# Honesty

is the first chapter
in the book of
wisdom.

Thomas Jefferson

To give anything
less than your best,
is to sacrifice
the **Gift.**

Steve Prefontaine

If you
**work hard**
and
you do your best,
you can do anything.

**Erin Heatherton**

A PROBLEM IS A CHANCE FOR YOU TO DO YOUR BEST.

Duke Ellington

# I'M JUST MYSELF.
## That's the best way to put it.

**Post Malone**

is the best prayer
that anyone could say.
I say that one a lot.
Thank you expresses
**EXTREME GRATITUDE,**
**HUMILITY,**
**UNDERSTANDING.**

**Alice Walker**

Don't let people disrespect you.

My mom says
don't open the door
to the devil.

Surround yourself with

## POSITIVE PEOPLE.

Cuba Gooding, Jr.

You need to be able to
## manage stress
because hard times will come,
and a positive outlook
is what gets you through.

**Marie Osmond**

Be true to yourself
and
surround yourself with positive,
supportive people.

**Payal Kadakia**

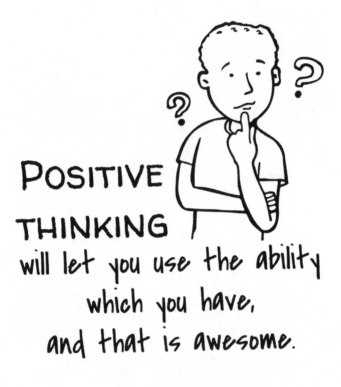

POSITIVE THINKING will let you use the ability which you have, and that is awesome.

**Zig Ziglar**

# Remind yourself
that the greatest technique
for bringing peace
into your life is
to always choose being **kind**
when you have a choice between
being right or being kind.

Wayne Dyer

The essential conditions
of everything you do must be

# CHOICE,

# LOVE,

# PASSION.

Nadia Boulanger

I was intelligent enough
to make up my own mind.
I not only had freedom of choice,
I had freedom of
**expression.**

**Amy Tan**

Our world is at the crossroads. We have a choice, right and wrong.

LL Cool J

If every choice you make
comes from an honest place,
you're solid,
and nothing anybody
can say about
you can rock you
or change your
opinion.

Angelina Jolie

I have the choice

of being

constantly active

and happy

or introspectively

passive and sad.

Sylvia Plath

TRUE HAPPINESS CONSISTS
NOT IN THE
MULTITUDE OF FRIENDS,
BUT IN THE
WORTH AND CHOICE.

Ben Jonson

There's going to be **stress** in life, but it's your choice whether to let it **affect** you or not.

Valerie Bertinelli

The remarkable thing is,
we have a choice
**everyday**
regarding the attitude
we will embrace
for that day.

Charles R. Swindoll

Often people ask
how I manage to be **happy**
despite having
no arms and no legs.
The quick answer is that
I have a choice.
I can be angry
about not having limbs,
or I can be thankful
that I have a purpose.
I choose gratitude.

**Nick Vujicic**

# Success

is a state of mind.
If you want success,
start thinking of yourself
as a success.

Joyce Brothers

Success is falling
nine times
and
getting up
ten.

Jon Bon Jovi

**Success** is the maximum utilization of the ability that you have.

Zig Ziglar

For me,
success is a state of mind.
I feel like success isn't about
**conquering something;**
it's being happy
with who you are.

**Britney Spears**

The most important thing is being **passionate** about what you're doing and always give it your all. That is the key to success.

**Charlie White**

Your success depends
mainly upon
what you think of yourself
and whether
**you believe
in
yourself.**

William J. H. Boetcker

A liar will not be believed, even when he speaks the truth.

Aesop

It's good to test yourself
and develop your
talents and ambitions
as fully as you can
and achieve greater success;
but I think success is the feeling
you get from a job
well done,
and the key thing is
to do the work.

**Peter Thiel**

Success is dependent on
# EFFORT

Sophocles

Before anything else,

**PREPARATION IS THE**

key

to success.

Alexander Graham Bell

Sometimes it's the **smallest decisions** that can change your life forever.

Keri Russell

# You can't change
who you are,
but you can change
what you have in your head,
you can refresh
what you're thinking about,
you can put
some fresh air in your brain.

**Ernesto Bertarelli**

Ask yourself:
Have you been kind today?
Make kindness your
daily modus operandi
and change your world.

**Annie Lennox**

If you **change** the way you look at things, the things you look at **change.**

**Wayne Dyer**

THE FIRST STEP TOWARD

# CHANGE

IS AWARENESS.
The second step is acceptance.

Nathaniel Branden

The only thing
that will make you happy is

# being happy

with who you are,
and not who
people think you are.

**Goldie Hawn**

Being happy

never goes out of style.

**Lilly Pulitzer**

# Believe in yourself!

# Have faith in your abilities!

## Without a humble

## but

reasonable confidence in your own powers

## you cannot be

## successful or happy.

**Norman Vincent Peale**

# Honesty
## is the best policy.

Benjamin Franklin

There are some things
you learn best
in calm,
and some
in storm.

**Willa Cather**

**Write it** on your heart that every day is the best day in the year.

Ralph Waldo Emerson

Whatever you want in life,
other people are going
to want it too.
Believe in yourself enough
to accept the idea
that you have
an equal right to it.

Diane Sawyer

Either
I will find a way,
or
I will make one.

Philip Sidney

A person who won't **READ** has no advantage over one who can't read.

**Mark Twain**

There are only two mistakes
one can make
along the road to truth;
not going all the way,
and not starting.

Buddha

# Every day
we have
plenty of opportunities
## to get angry,
## stressed or offended.
But what you're doing
when you indulge

these **negative emotions**
are giving something outside
yourself power
over your happiness.
You can choose to not let

little things **upset you.**

Joel Osteen

The most beautiful thing
you can wear is

CONFIDENCE.

Blake Lively

*If you fell down yesterday,*

## STAND UP TODAY.

H. G. Wells

When you practice
gratefulness,
there is a sense of respect
toward others.

Dalai Lama

Study nature,
love nature,
stay close to nature.

*It will*

*never fail you.*

Frank Lloyd Wright

Nothing you wear is
more important than your

smile

**Connie Stevens**

**Smile** in the mirror.
Do that every morning
and you'll start to see
a **big difference** in your life.

Yoko Ono

The most wasted of all days is
one without

## LAUGHTER.

e. e. cummings

# REACH FOR THE STARS

Christa McAuliffe

# Excellence

is doing ordinary things
extraordinarily well.

John W. Gardner

# EXCELLENCE
IS A CONTINUOUS PROCESS
AND NOT AN
## ACCIDENT.

A. P. J. Abdul Kalam

**Productivity** is never an accident. It is always the result of a commitment to excellence, intelligent planning, and **focused effort.**

Paul J. Meyer

So many times,
  people told me
I can't do this or can't do that.
*My nature is that
I don't listen very well.*
I'm very determined,
and I believe in myself.
My parents brought me up that way.
Thank God for that.
I don't let anything stand in my way.

**Chantal Sutherland**

Great minds
        discuss ideas;
average minds
        discuss events;
small minds

discuss people.

**Eleanor Roosevelt**

I've learned that people will forget what you **said,** people will forget what you **did,** but people will never forget how you made them **feel.**

Maya Angelou

Research is creating new **knowledge.**

Neil Armstrong

You just don't know in life.
Life knocks you
about and pushes you
over boundaries.
But be ready.
Do your homework;
that's all I can say.

**Julie Andrews**

I will not go into a story
unprepared.
I will do my **homework**,
and that's something
I learned at an early age.

**Ed Bradley**

# IF YOU TELL THE
# TRUTH,
## YOU DON'T HAVE TO REMEMBER
## ANYTHING.

Mark Twain

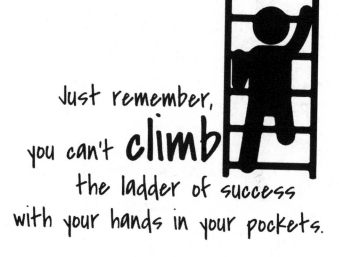

Just remember, you can't **climb** the ladder of success with your hands in your pockets.

Arnold Schwarzenegger

We learned about honesty
and integrity - that
the truth matters...
that you don't take shortcuts
or play by your own
set of rules...
and success doesn't count
unless you earn it fair and square.

**Michelle Obama**

Success isn't always about greatness.
It's about consistency.
Consistent hard work
leads to success.
Greatness will come.

**Dwayne Johnson**

You go through
life wondering
what is it all about
but at the end of the day
it's all about

# family.

**Rod Stewart**

I absolutely **love** spending time with my family.

Kevin Alejandro

I think **togetherness** is a very important ingredient to family life.

Barbara Bush

The most important thing
in the world is
*family and love.*

John Wooden

Be sure of yourself,
don't let anyone bully you,
be a strong and independent
woman or boy.

Nicole Polizzi

**Older people** sit down and ask, 'What is it?' but the boy asks, 'What can I do with it?'.

Steve Jobs

# FEELING GRATITUDE
and not expressing
it is like wrapping
a present
and not giving it.

William Arthur Ward

I have a lot
to be grateful for.

**Annie Lennox**

FOCUS

on the
positives
and be grateful.

Katrina Bowden

When you are grateful - when you can see what you have - you unlock blessings to flow in your life.

Suze Orman

BE GRATEFUL FOR
WHAT YOU HAVE
AND
STOP COMPLAINING
IT BORES
EVERYBODY ELSE,
DOES YOU NO GOOD,
AND DOESN'T SOLVE
ANY PROBLEMS.

Zig Ziglar

Every day,
I like to **wake up**
and remind myself
to be grateful of the
simple things.

Miranda Kerr

So every single day, I found **something** to be grateful for and that's a powerful lesson.

**Alice Barrett**

Never forget that
the most powerful force on earth is

# LOVE

Nelson Rockefeller

THE DREAMS AND PASSIONS
STORED WITHIN HEARTS
ARE

POWERFUL

KEYS

WHICH CAN UNLOCK

A WEALTH OF POTENTIAL.

John C. Maxwell

# Forgive more, Love more, Communicate often.

Adaeze A.E

If you're smart,
you'll always be humble.
ou can learn all you want,
but there'll always be

# Somebody

who's never read a book
who'll know twice
what you know.

**David Duchovny**

Intelligence
is the ability to adapt
to change.

Stephen Hawking

Talent wins games,
but
teamwork and intelligence
wins

# championships.

**Michael Jordan**

# Tough times

## never last, but tough people Do.

Robert H. Schuller

# FAILURE

is simply the opportunity to begin again. this time more intelligently.

**Henry Ford**

You may not control all the **events** that happen to you, but you can decide **not to be** reduced by them.

Maya Angelou

The language of friendship
is not words
but meanings.

Henry David Thoreau

# Kindness

is the language
which the deaf can hear
and the blind can see.

**Mark Twain**

# A #2 PENCIL AND A DREAM CAN TAKE YOU ANYWHERE.

Joyce Meyer

Nothing great in the world
has ever been accomplished
without
## PASSION.

ABGeorg Wilhelm Friedrich Hegel

We focus
so much on our differences,
and that is creating,
I think,
a lot of chaos and negativity
and bullying in the world.
And I think
if everybody focused
on what we all have
in common - which is - we all want
to be happy.

Ellen DeGeneres

If we cannot
now end our differences,
at least we can help
make the world
safe for diversity.

John F. Kennedy

To be yourself in a world
that is constantly trying
to make you
something else
is the GREATEST

ACCOMPLISHMENT.

**Ralph Waldo Emerson**

An eye for an eye
only ends up
making the whole world

BLIND.

Mahatma Gandhi

Every GREAT DREAM

begins with a dreamer.
Always remember,
you have within you the strength,
the patience,
and the passion
to reach for the stars
to change the **WORLD**.

**Harriet Tubman**

The secret of success
is constancy to
purpose.

Benjamin Disraeli

We are what we repeatedly do.

# EXCELLENCE,
then,

# IS NOT AN ACT,

# BUT A HABIT.

**Will Durant**

**Success** consists of getting up just one more time than you fall.

Oliver Goldsmith

The only place **success** comes before **work** is in the dictionary.

Vince Lombardi

Success is
**getting what you want.**
Happiness is
**wanting what you get.**

Dale Carnegie

# 4

Four things for success:

## WORK AND PRAY, THINK AND BELIEVE.

Norman Vincent Peale

Many of life's **failures** are people who did not realize how **close** they were to success when they gave up.

Thomas A. Edison

Action is
the foundational key
to all success.

Pablo Picasso

Try to look at your
weakness and convert it into
your strength.

That's success.

**Zig Ziglar**

The starting point of all achievement is Desire.

Napoleon Hill

The secret
of your success is
determined by
your daily agenda.

John C. Maxwell

# PATIENCE, PERSISTENCE AND PERSPIRATION

make an unbeatable
combination
for success.

Napoleon Hill

# Kindness

in words creates confidence.

# Kindness

in thinking creates profoundness.

# Kindness

in giving creates love.

Lao Tzu

Go **EMPOWER** yourself.
You need confidence
because the one thing tha
bullying does is it belittles you,
and it takes away
your confidence,
and nobody
deserves that.

**Bill Goldberg**

I realized that

# BULLYING

never has to do with you.
It's the bully who's insecure.

**Shay Mitchell**

# People
### like to be around those who give off

# positive energy.

**Erin Heatherton**

I've learned from
**experience**
that if you work harder at it,
and apply more energy
and time to it,
and more consistency,
you get a better result.
It comes from the work.

Louis C. K.

Feeling **sorry** for ourselves
is the most useless
waste of energy on the planet.
It does absolutely no good.
We can't let our circumstances
or what others do or
don't do control us.
We can decide to be happy regardless.

**Joyce Meyer**

# Energy & persistence

## CONQUER ALL THINGS.

Benjamin Franklin

Choose to **focus** your time, energy and conversation around people who inspire you, support you and help you to grow you into your happiest, strongest, wisest self.

Karen Salmansohn

Most of us **start** out
with a positive attitude
and
a plan to do our best.

Marilu Henner

My dear friend,
clear your mind of

# CANT

Samuel Johnson

the negative;
accentuate the positive!

Donna Karan

# Believe

THAT LIFE IS WORTH LIVING

AND

YOUR BELIEF WILL HELP

CREATE THE FACT.

William James

# A positive attitude

can really make dreams
come true
it did for me.

David Bailey

Social media is a superimposing place where people are usually

BRAGGING.

Brandon Stanton

I don't live my life
seeking validation from
people on **social media.**

Ricki-Lee Coulter

**WHAT IS INTERESTING IS** THE POWER AND THE IMPACT OF **SOCIAL MEDIA...** SO WE MUST TRY TO USE SOCIAL MEDIA IN A GOOD WAY.

Malala Yousafzai

# Social media is
## an amazing tool,
## but it's really
the face-to-face interaction
## that makes
## a long-term impact.

Felicia Day

It takes discipline
not to let social media
steal your time.

Alexis Ohanian

THE GREATEST GLORY IN

# LIVING LIES

NOT IN NEVER FALLING,

BUT IN

# RISING

EVERY TIME WE FALL.

Ralph Waldo Emerson

Time is not measured by
the passing of years
but by
what one does,
what one feels,
and what one achieves.

Jawaharlal Nehru

It's so important
to realize that every time

**you get upset,**

it drains your emotional energy.
Losing your cool makes you tired.
Getting angry a lot messes with
your health.

**Joyce Meyer**

Success is simple.
Do what's right,
the right way,
at the
right time.

**Arnold H. Glasow**

The TIME is
always right
to do what is
RIGHT.

Martin Luther King, Jr.

The two most powerful warriors are

# PATIENCE AND TIME.

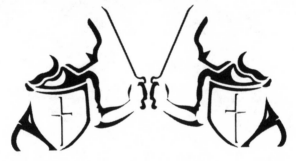

**Leo Tolstoy**

Instead of **hating,**
I have chosen to forgive
and spend all of
my positive energy
on CHANGING THE WORLD.

Camryn Manheim

# FORGIVE

## THOSE WHO HAVE HURT YOU.

Les Brown

It's one of the greatest gifts you can give yourself, to **FORGIVE.** Forgive everybody.

Maya Angelou

The weak can never forgive.
# Forgiveness
is the attribute of the strong.

**Mahatma Gandhi**

# THEY INVENTED HUGS TO LET PEOPLE KNOW

## YOU **LOVE** THEM WITHOUT SAYING ANYTHING.

Bil Keane

**Don't** go around saying the world owes you a living. The world owes you nothing. It was here first.

Mark Twain

No one should be ashamed
to admit they are **wrong,**
which is but saying,
in other words,
that they are wiser **today**
than they were yesterday.

Alexander Pope

Some people think
that you have to be
the LOUDEST voice in the room
to make a difference.
That is just not true.
Often,
the best thing
we can do is
turn down the volume.
When the sound is quieter,
you can actually hear
what someone else is saying.
And that can make a world of
difference.

**Nikki Haley**

# Kind words

do not cost much.
Yet they accomplish much.

Blaise Pascal

# GOSSIP

IS THE ART OF SAYING
NOTHING
IN A WAY
THAT LEAVES PRACTICALLY
NOTHING UNSAID.

Walter Winchell

# People gossip.

People are insecure,
so they talk about other people
so that they won't be talked about.
They point out flaws
in other people to make them
feel good about themselves.
I think at any age or any social class,
that's present.

Blake Lively

# I HAVE LEARNED

THAT THERE IS MORE POWER

IN A **GOOD STRONG HUG**

THAN

IN A THOUSAND MEANINGFUL

WORDS.

Ann Hood

# PEOPLE MAY HEAR YOUR WORDS, BUT THEY FEEL YOUR ATTITUDE.

John C. Maxwell

There's no point
in saying anything but the

# TRUTH

**Amy Winehouse**

It is just as cowardly
to judge an
absent person as it is wicked
to strike a defenseless one.
Only the ignorant
and narrow-minded gossip,
for they speak of persons
instead of things.

Lawrence G. Lovasik

# Lead the life
that will make you
kindly and friendly
to everyone about you,
and you will be surprised
what a happy life you will lead.

Charles M. Schwab

# If you are happy,
you can give happiness.
If you don't love yourself
and if you are unhappy
with yourself,
you can't give anything else
but that.

Gisele Bundchen

Be happy with what you have and are, be generous with both, and you won't have to hunt for happiness.

**William E. Gladstone**

I gave up my struggle
with perfection a long time ago.
That is a concept
I don't find very interesting anymore.
Everyone just wants to look good
in the photographs.
I think that is where
some of the pressure comes from.

# Be happy.
# Be yourself,
the day is about a lot more.

Anne Hathaway

To be **happy,**
it first takes being comfortable
being in your own shoes.
The rest can work up from there.

**Sophia Bush**